HOW TO LIVE WITH A NEUROTIC HUSBAND

Also by Stephen Baker and available from New English Library
HOW TO LIVE WITH A NEUROTIC WIFE
GAMES DOGS PLAY

By Stephen Baker and Eric Gurney
HOW TO LIVE WITH A NEUROTIC DOG

By Eric Gurney
HOW TO LIVE WITH A CALCULATING CAT
THE CALCULATING CAT RETURNS

How to Live with a Neurotic Husband

NEW ENGLISH LIBRARY/TIMES MIRROR

First published in Great Britain in 1971 by New English Library Ltd

First NEL Paperback Edition October 1972
New edition October 1974
New edition December 1977
This new edition September 1980

NEL Books are published by
New English Library Limited,
Barnard's Inn, Holborn,
London EC1N 2JR.

Made and printed in Great Britain by

Hunt Barnard Web Offset Ltd, Aylesbury

0 450 04973 6

Contents

1
WHAT MAKES A HUSBAND NEUROTIC

Husbands become neurotic when they discover that – like so many of their married friends – they have a wife. The thought occurs to them soon after the wedding, usually the morning after as the effect of champagne begins to wear off. The discovery leaves them in a state of shock.

It is easy to see why this should be so. The nuptial ceremony in itself is a traumatic experience for the male participant, especially if he is going through it only for the first, second, or third time in his life, and is still a novice at it. The event marks the end of his former, more wholesome way of life. Contrary to his natural inclinations, he is now asked to stay with the same female companion for months, or even years at a time. The notion appears to have considerable appeal to the bride, and her parents. But not to the groom. More than anyone else, he realizes the future consequences of his action.

Before wedding: As a bachelor, his arrival at a party would attract the attention of female guests who would surround

him immediately. He could freely talk to them and take his time conducting a survey before taking action.

After wedding: Appearing with his spouse (see couple second from left), male visitor finds that his appeal to the opposite

Male reaction to female guests shows up in electrocardiogram (above). Vigorous heart activity (A) is symptomatic of bachelor enjoying himself at a party. It slows down (B) once he is married.

sex has now considerably diminished. His activities are inhibited by his wife who not at all shares his social interests.

Her husband's detailed and oft-repeated stories notwithstanding, the average wife often fails to appreciate the things he had to give up to get married. Here is a partial* list:

KEYS TO SEVERAL APARTMENTS

PICTURES OF GIRLFRIENDS

TELEPHONE CALLS AT 4 A.M.

ALL-NIGHT PARTIES

MOTORCYCLE

DIRTY SOCKS

DUTCH TREATS

EMPTY BEER CANS ON THE FLOOR

* A more complete list: Abigail, Amelia, Amy, Anatola, Augusta, Belle, Beth, Bonnie, Camilla, Caroline, Chloe, Clara, Claudia, Colette, Cynthia, Daisy, Dale, Davina, Deborah, Delphine, Diana, Dolores, Donna, Dorothy, Drusilla, Duloie, Esther, Eunice, Eva, Faith, Fay, Felicia, Flavie, Floria, Frances, Freda, Frederica, Gabrielle, Gail, Genevieve, Gladys, Guinevere, Gwendolyn, Hannah, Harriet, Hatti, Hazel, Hedda, Helga, Herta, Hildegarde, Holly, Hope, Hortense, Ianthe, Ida, Ilsa, Ina, Inez, Iona, Iris, Irma, Isadora, Jane, Jasmine, Jean, Jessica, Jill, Josephine, Joy, Judith, Julia, Katherine, Kay, Kim, Kitty, Lana, Laura, Lena, Lesley, Libey, Linda, Louise, Lucy, Lynn, Mabel, Margaret, Martha, Martina, Maria, Marsha, Mary, Melissa, Milly, Mona, Muriel, Myrtle, Nelly, Nola, Odette, Olga, Ophelia, Penelope, Priscilla, Prudence, Quinta, Rachel, Rebecca, Rita, Sabina, Selma, Shirley, Sophia, Sylvia, Thelma, Valeria, Vera, Veronica, Violet, Vivian, Wendy.

Replacing the girls he has known as a bachelor are women with a more mature sense of responsibility. They prove – just what his wife keeps telling him – that looks are not everything.

Girlfriend – as she appeared to him *before* marrying her.

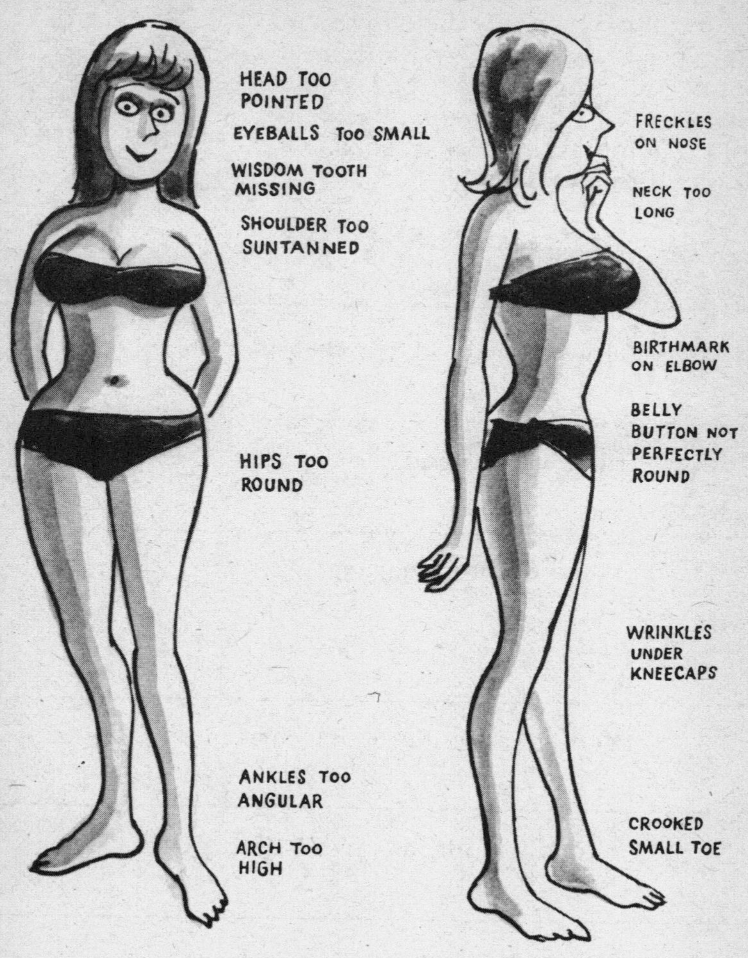

The same girl – as she appears to him after marrying her. Husband soon must learn to accept the fact that married life is but a series of compromises. Flaws in the wife's character become more obvious after a while.

It appears to men that their spouse's disposition, too, changes shortly after the wedding. As a wife, her interest in him is not as deep as it appeared before marriage. Even her polite inquiries – as, for example, when he comes home in the evening – have a different ring to them now.

HER STATEMENTS

How was your day in the office, dear?

I like your friend.

You look tired, darling.

You are a wonderful dancer.

Would you like a cup of coffee?

Let's make love.

Don't forget your overcoat, dear.

HIS THOUGHTS (as a bachelor)	**HIS THOUGHTS (as a husband)**
She is interested in my career.	How much does she know about Mabel?
She likes my friends.	I wonder why she likes him.
So kind, so understanding.	All right, so the lines in my face are showing. She is not getting any younger either.
She is kind enough not to tell me the truth.	The liar.
That's just what I need.	Too lazy to mix a cocktail, eh?
Hallelujah!	Can't she see I had a hard day in the office?
She cares about me.	Nag, nag, nag, nag, nag, nag.

Included in every family plan is the dreamhouse built to live in happily ever after. Before the wedding, couple come to an agreement as to size and appearance of the home.

The real thing is nothing like the dream. Additional space is needed as family grows. As rooms multiply, so do mortgage payments.

Soon, the husband discovers that all his divorced friends – without exceptions – were married at one time or another. This information does not improve his present state of mind. It is not the possible departure of his wife that concerns him (he could easily survive that) but the amount of money her leaving would cost him.

Fortunately — and you can thus inform your husband to soothe his anxieties – he has nothing to worry about. Marriage laws in the USA are such that both parties receive the same treatment in case of divorce. Especially the wife. The amount of alimony depends solely on her needs and his earning capacity. For example, a man who earns ten thousand dollars a year rarely is asked to pay more than that to his estranged wife. In most states, there are also laws to protect either spouse's property rights. The wife gets the house, furniture, car, custody of children, stock and bonds, and other support necessary for bare survival but the husband is permitted to keep everything else; that is, mortgage, cost of bringing up the children, interest payments, and all the neck-ties that he brought to the marriage.

His:
Hers:
$

2
HOW TO RECOGNIZE A NEUROTIC HUSBAND

To deal with your neurotic husband effectively – in fact, to deal with him at all – you must be able to recognize the symptoms of his problem.

The symptoms may be so slight that they escape cursory observation. Fortunately, you are near to him most of the time and thus in a position to know more about his behaviour pattern than any other person. Watch for the signs, superficial as they may appear at first glance. For example, if your husband screams from the top of his lungs, bangs his fists on the floor, tears the carpet, throws heavy objects* across the room, habitually jumps off the roof of skyscrapers, you may correctly surmise that his calm exterior notwithstanding, deep down inside something is bothering him.

*Living room couch, dining table, grand piano, his dog, his wife.

Eye movements of married man indicate alertness, quick reflex action. He is able to observe girls on the street, beach, and in the office without moving his head. Alone with his wife at home, particularly after several years of marriage, his eyeballs come to a standstill.

Rearview mirror enables driver to keep pedestrian traffic under close surveillance while keeping his car under control, more or less.

Holding his wife in a tight, loving embrace, husband obstructs her view of dance floor; this helps him in striking up new friendships without interference.

Reading newspaper in his favourite armchair gives husband an opportunity to keep up with latest developments.

Not wanting to arouse his wife's suspicion by turning and twisting his head, husband walks backward to get a better view of passing scenery.

Husband's private study – personally decorated by him – shows his reluctance to face up to the harsh realities of life;

namely, that in a monogamous society such as ours, the male can legally live with only one female at a time.

DOLORES

Mumbling in his sleep, man gives his wife a chance to learn about his true emotional needs.

Concerned about the impression he makes on the opposite sex,* neurotic husband stops frequently in front of mirror to inspect his bulging arms and shoulders, but – at the same time – ignoring his bulging waistline.

* his wife not included.

To keep in shape, the neurotic husband may insist on getting his exercise whenever – and wherever – he can.

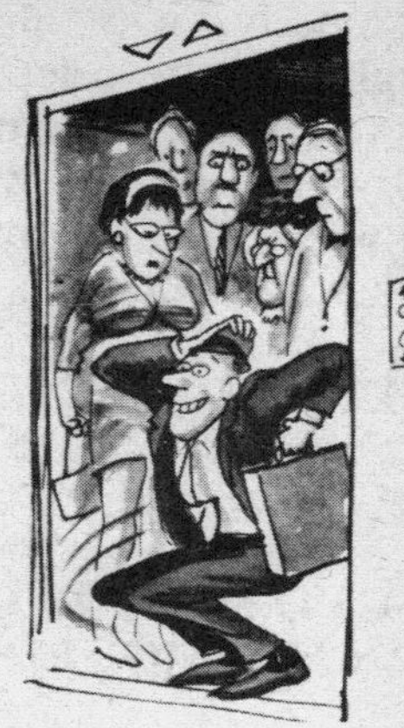

Deep-knee bends strengthen leg muscles.

Jogging makes use of muscles all over the body, except the head.

Occasionally, you may find that your husband is going through periods of depression, lasting anywhere from a few hours to sixty or seventy years at a time. Do not be alarmed. All he needs is your sympathy. You must of course understand what causes him to suffer so profoundly. He has good reasons. For example:

HE GAINED A POUND.

HE LOST A POUND.

HE SOLD SOME SECURITIES ON THE MARKET WHEN HE SHOULDN'T HAVE.

HE DIDN'T SELL SOME SECURITIES ON THE MARKET WHEN HE SHOULD HAVE.

HIS LIGHTER FAILED.

HIS CIGAR WENT OUT.

A TEENAGE GIRL ADDRESSED HIM RESPECTFULLY AS "SIR".

HE MISSED A PUTT ON THE EIGHTEENTH HOLE.

HE HAS A HANGOVER.

YOU CHANGED YOUR MIND ABOUT VISITING YOUR SISTER IN CLEVELAND.

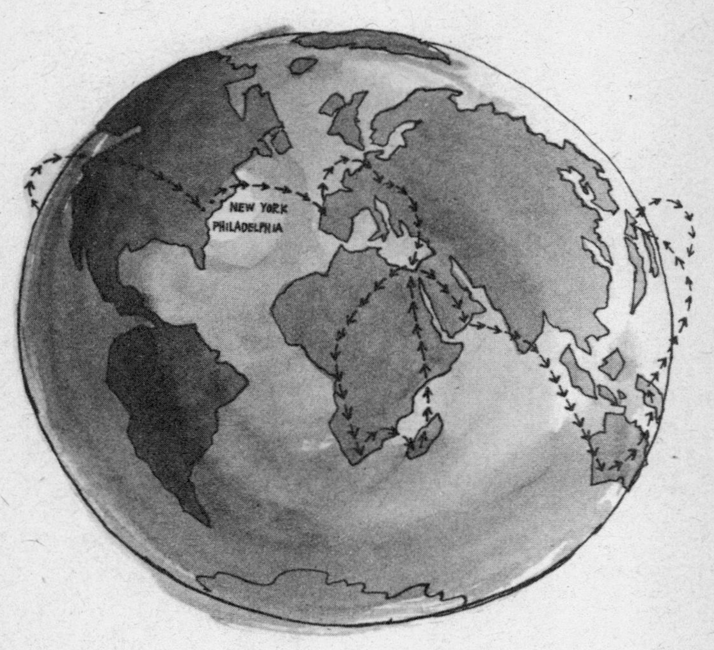

Your husband may not be as much in a hurry to get home as you think. Check his itinerary of his last business trip and see for yourself.

3
THE NEUROTIC HUSBAND AND HIS WORK

To a man, work is one of the most important parts in life. His business gives him the best excuse yet to stay away from home for days, or possibly for several weeks.

It wasn't always like that. There was a time when a man did not have to work for a living. There was a more practical approach to supporting a family. It was the wife's responsibility to cultivate the land, collect firewood, tan animal skins, stitch, weave, wash, tend to the children, feed the dog, put out the garbage, and tote heavy objects on top of her head. His responsibilities included sitting before his hut and supervising the proceedings. This arrangement had certain advantages; much was being accomplished without his having to get up, except to go to the bathroom.

However, with the advancement of civilization came all kinds of reform. Women learned to read and write. And so they began to ask questions. It was at this point that husbands had enough. Recognizing the need for preventive action, they banded together to look for places away from home. They erected office buildings and factories for that purpose and established the so-called nine-to-five working routine.

This, of course, did not wholly relieve women from their chores. Only the nature of their responsibilities has changed. The new ones were equally strenuous. Now it was their function to listen to their husband's complaints in the evening returning from work.

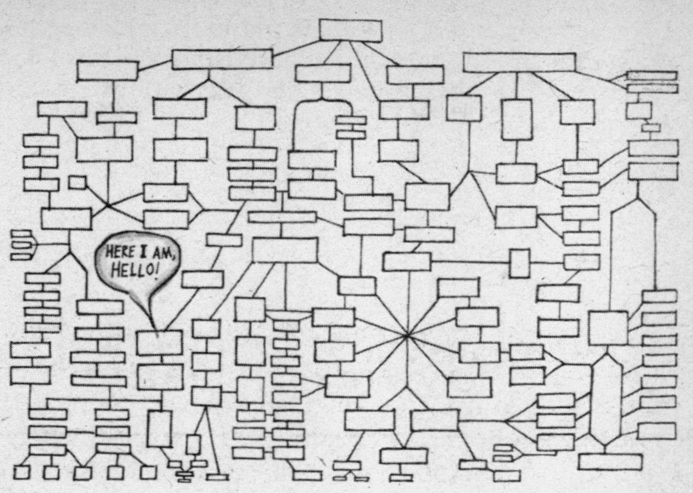

Stories about office politics – as related by the husband – may confuse a wife at first. To be able to follow his daily reports she must learn to understand the basic structure of the corporation for which he works. Ask him to draw you an organization chart. If nothing else, this will help you to understand why you are confused.

Husband's description of his superiors enables listeners to have a mental image of them and appreciate what – and who – he is up against from 9 a.m. to 5 p.m.

As a shrewd observer of human nature, a husband lets nothing escape his attention about his business associates. He is not a man to be fooled. Some of his observations are shown below:

THE PERSON	HIS GOOD QUALITIES	HIS BAD QUALITIES
 J. W. Chairman of the Board		Too conservative. Thinks too much about corporate profits. Overly friendly. His earlobes are too large. Overpaid.
 K. T. President		Laughs too much. Stays in the office too late in the evenings. Comes in too early in the morning, setting up a bad example. Overpaid.
 P. L. Executive Vice President		Too much of an intellectual. Too polite. His office has four windows instead of three. Overpaid.

THE PERSON	HIS GOOD QUALITIES	HIS BAD QUALITIES
 N. F. Treasurer		Doesn't look like an executive. A teetotaler. His secretary is in love with him but he is too busy to pay attention to her. Overpaid.
 L. O. Office Manager		Too conscientious. Reads too many books. His office has one window instead of none. Overpaid.
 S. D. Comptroller	Signs paychecks.	Too honest. Overpaid.
 L. K. Sales Manager		Takes his job too seriously. Works too hard. Has a big nose. Overpaid.

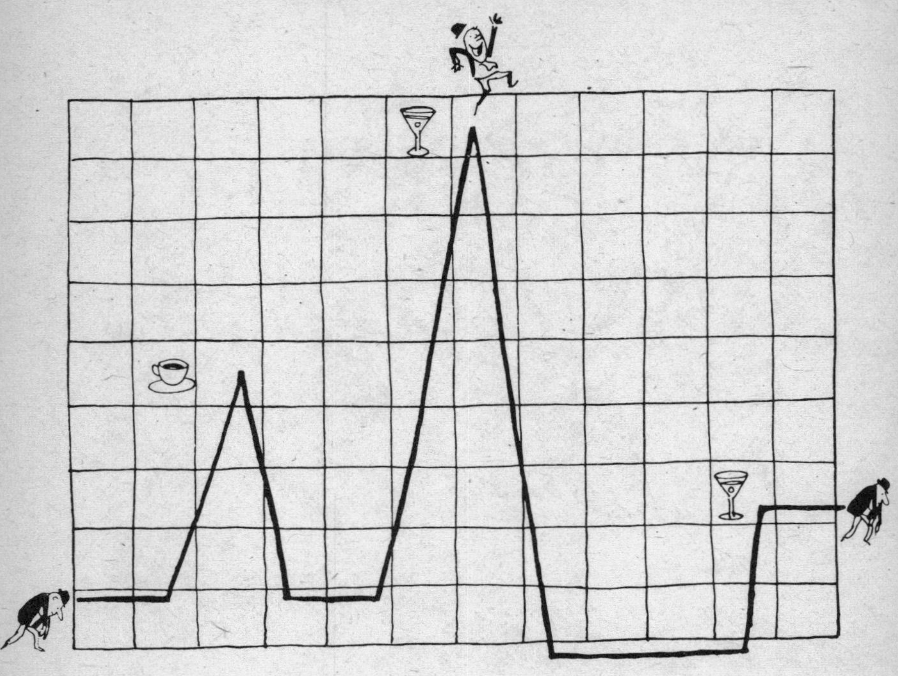

Metabolism chart shows fluctuation in energy during office hours. His vitality low in the morning as husband arrives at the office and promptly goes back to sleep in desk chair, it perks up at coffee break. Fatigued by the effort of stirring coffee and lifting the cup to his lip, he takes a short nap before lunch. During noon, his disposition improves markedly as he consumes his daily ration – five to seven – cocktails with his meal. He manages to find his way back to his office. Here, secretary wakes him up at five o'clock. His strength regained, husband now leaves the office and heads for nearest bar.

Friends in the bar car on his way home help commuting husband to work off his inner tensions.

There are times when your husband needs a few encouraging words. Recite a poem or two to him when he goes off to work in the morning. Here are a few you can use:

Early to bed
Early to rise
Makes a man healthy, wealthy and wise.

(Proverb)

A man of words, and not of deeds,
Is like a garden full of weeds.

(Proverb)

If a task is once begun
Never leave it till it's done.
Be the labour great or small,
Do it well or not at all.

(Anonymous)

When things go wrong, as they sometimes will,
When the road you're trudging seems all up hill,
When the funds are low and the debts are high,
And you want to smile, but you have to sigh,
When care is pressing you down a bit,
Rest, if you must – but don't you quit.

(Unknown)

Good for the body is the work of the body,
good for the soul the work of the soul, and
good for either the work of the other.

(Proverb)

Who reasons wisely is not therefore wise;
His pride in reasoning, not in acting, lies.

(Proverb)

A cool mouth, and warm feet, live long.

(Proverb)

Today is ours; what do we fear?
Today is ours; we have it here.
Let's treat it kindly, that it may
Wish, at least, with us to stay.
Let's banish business, banish sorrow;
To the gods belongs tomorrow.

(Proverb)

Let your precept be, "Be easy."

(Proverb)

Tomorrow is a new day.

(Proverb)

Things at first hard and rough, are by use made tender and gentle.

(Proverb)

To everything its use.

(Proverb)

Be wiser than other people if you can; but do not tell them so.

(Proverb)

Work is the sustenance of noble minds.

(Proverb)

The greater the difficulty, the greater the glory.

(Proverb)

Do noble things, not dream them.

(Proverb)

Give your husband a warm welcome when he comes home in the evening. He needs your sympathy. **(1)** Offer him a strong shoulder **(2)** on which he can lean. On his way to the other

end of the room, lower him gradually to the floor **(3),** then prop him up into an upright sitting position **(4)** in his armchair.

Waiting for his meal, your husband will change positions several times. Wake him up gently at dinner time – if you can.

A drink will do him good.

If you are a business executive's wife, your role as a helping mate becomes even more important. Now, more than ever, you must understand what he must go through every day to keep his position.

His life is not an easy one. As a prominent member of the business community, he must do what is expected from leaders in industry like him. He must drink harder to keep up with all his friends who also must drink harder to keep up with him. He must be willing to assume the awesome responsibility of hiring a secretary and supervise her conduct not only during business hours but far into the night. And that isn't all. Being on an expense account, he must now decide where, what, and how much to eat.

In order to be a good wife to such a man – and not to embarrass him – you should know a little about his work so that you can carry on at least a simple, cursory conversation with the people he brings home to dinner. Fortunately, this should be no problem for anyone willing to take a few minutes now and then to scan a small selected list of trade journals and books* elemental to understanding the world of business.

*ABERLE, JOHN W., and others. *General Business for Today and Tomorrow*
ANDERSON, CHESTER R., and others. *Business reports*
ANSHEN, MELVIN. *Introduction to Business*
APPLEMAN, JOHN A. *How to Increase Your Money-making Power*
AUSLANDER, M. ARTHUR. *How to Profit From and Protect Your Business Ideas*
AUSLANDER, M. ARTHUR. *How to Protect Your Business Ideas*
BALDWIN, SUMMERFIELD. *Business in the Middle Ages*
BEACH, LESLIE, and E. L. CLARK. *Psychology in Business*
BEARD, MIRIAM. *History of Business*, 2 vols.
BICKHAM, GEORGE. *Universal Penman*
BONNEVILLE, JOSEPH H., and others. *Organizing and Financing Business*
BOVET, ERIC D. *Dynamics of Business Motivation*
BOYS SCOUTS OF AMERICA. *American Business*
BRANDEIS, LOUIS D. *Business: A profession*
BRIDGES, FRANCIS J., and K. W. OLM, *Business policy: Cases, Incidents, and Readings*
BROADWAY, FRANK. *Management Problems of Expansion*
BROWN, LELAND. *Effective Business Report Writing*
BURSK, EDWARD C. and others. *World of Business*, 4 vols.
CARR, ALBERT Z., *Business as a Game*
CHEIT, EARL F. *Business Establishment*
CLARK, JOHN M. *Social Control of Business*
COLBERG, MARSHALL R., and others. *Business Economics: Principles and Cases*
COLLIER, J. *Effective Long Range Business Planning*
CRABBE, ERNEST H., and others. *General Business*

DEAGLIO, MARIO. *Private Enterprise and Public Emulation*

DEVLIN, FRANK J. *Progress Guide and Workbook to Accompany Business Communication*

DURAND, ROBERT. *Business: Its Organization, Management and Responsibilities*

DYER, FREDERICK C., and others. *Putting Yourself Over in Business*

BELLS, RICHARD, and CLARENCE WALTON. *Conceptual Foundations of Business*

FENN, D. JR., and others. *Business Decision Making and Government Policy: Cases in Business and Government*

FRENCH, ROBERT W., and BERNARD H. BAUM. *Basics for Business*

FRITZ, N. *Introductory Business Practice: A Practice Set for General Business and Clerical Students*

GENTRY, DWIGHT L., and C. A. TAFF. *Elements of Business Enterprise*

GERAY, HERBERT. *Background of Business*

GERSTENBERG, CHARLES W. *Financial Organization and Management of Business*

GIBBONS, JOHN F. *Basic Facts of Business*

GLOS, RAYMOND E., and HAROLD A. BAKER. *Introduction to Business*

GRAS, N. S. B., and H. M. LARSON. *Casebook in American Business History*

GREENWOOD, FRANK. *Casebook for Management and Business Policy: A Systems Approach*

HADLEY, G. *Introduction to Business Statistics*

HALSEY, GEORGE D. *How to Achieve Success and Happiness in Business*

HART, DONALD J. *Business in a Dynamic Society*

HASTINGS, PAUL G. *Fundamentals of Business Enterprise*

JANIS, J. HAROLD. *Business Communication Reader*

JOSEPHS, RAY. *Streamlining Your Executive Workload*

JUCIUS, MICHAEL J., and G. R. TERRY. *Introduction to Business*

KEITH, LYMAN A., and C. E. GUBELLINI. *Introduction to Business Enterprise*

LARSEN, SPENCER A., ed. *How to Improve Business Communications*

LASSER, JACOB K. *Executive's Guide to Business Procedures*

LIEBERS, ARTHUR. *Key to Successful Business*

LYONS, IVORY, and M. ZYMELMAN. *Economic Analysis of the Firm*

MCGUIRE, JOSEPH W. *Business and Society*

MCQUIRE, JOSEPH W. *Theories of Business Behaviour*

METCALF, HENRY C., and L. URWICK, eds. *Dynamic Administration*

MILLS, FREDERICK C. *Statistical Methods*

MINRATH, WILLIAM R. *How to Run Your Own Business and Make It Pay*

MUSSELMAN, VERNON A., and EUGENE HUGHES. *Introduction to Modern Business*

NANASSY, L., and C. FANCHER. *General Business and Economic Understandings*

NATIONAL BUSINESS EDUCATION ASSOCIATION. *Selected Readings in Business and Office Occupations*

NEWMAN, WILLIAM H., and JAMES P. LOGAN. *Business Policies and Central Management*

O'SHAUGHNESSY, J. *Business Organization*

OWENS, RICHARD N. *Introduction to Business Policy*

PETERSON, ELMORE, and others. *Business Organization and Management*

PRATHER, CHARLES L. *Financing Business Firms*

PRICE, RAY, and others. *General Business for Everyday Living*

RAYMOND, THOMAS C. *Problems in Business Administration*

RIGGLEMAN, JOHN R., and IRA N. FRISBEE. *Business Statistics*

ROBINSON, EDWIN, and J. C. HALL. *College Business Organization and Management*

SAVAGE, WILLIAM G., and others. *Business Review for Professional Secretaries*

SHILT, BERNARD A., and others. *Business Principles and Management*

SIELAFF, THEODORE J., and JOHN W. ABERLE. *Introduction to Business*

SIELAFF, THEODORE J., and P. S. WANG. *Practical Problems in Business and Economic Statistics*

SIMONDS, ROLLIN H., and others. *Business Administration: Problems and Functions*

SPENGLER, EDWIN H., and JACOB KLEIN. *Introduction to Business*

SPRIEGEL, WILLIAM. *Principles of Business Organization and Operation*

Help your husband entertain his clients. Make sure everyone enjoys the party.

Be nice to his boss.

4
THE NEUROTIC HUSBAND AND HIS MONEY

Men often try to overcome their feelings of insecurity by accumulating worldly possessions. Unconsciously they believe that a lot of money in the bank will make most of their problems disappear, including perhaps the biggest one of all, the wife.

That hope motivates many husbands to work hard, and in some cases, even achieve a state of solvency. The idea of being rich has its undeniable appeals; for example, a man of means can offer his wife a number of plausible alibis for not coming home in the evening. He can even afford to have a third person, such as a secretary, place a routine telephone call to his home, informing the waiting spouse that he expects to be busy that night. Such delegation of responsibilities permits him to concentrate fully on his various outside, wide-ranging financial enterprises, such as a mistress at the other side of town.

Be that as it may, a husband is still only as good as the wife who stands behind him. Your husband still needs you, his financial manipulations notwithstanding. For example, he may want to know mundane details about his finances like where the money for groceries is going to come from at the end of the month, will his telephone service be disconnected, etc. It is up to you to have that kind of information available to him.

To make him the financial success he wants to be, you must of course do your part in economizing at home. In your own small way, there is much you can do. You can go barefooted, pass up your vacation, walk to work, stake a goat in the backyard to provide milk for the family, make dresses out of potato sacks, and use warm water only if you really need it.

The itch-to-get-rich is a common psychosomatic disturbance perhaps best explained in the diagram above. Thinking about the unlimited business opportunities in this country, man's brain sends messages to various parts of his anatomy creating itching sensations at the top of his head **(1)**, tip of his nose **(2)**, his belly button **(3)**, feet **(4)**, and, through a sympathetic nervous system, behind his dog's ears (**5**). Scratching relaxes the sufferer and makes him believe ever so much more in his money-making scheme.

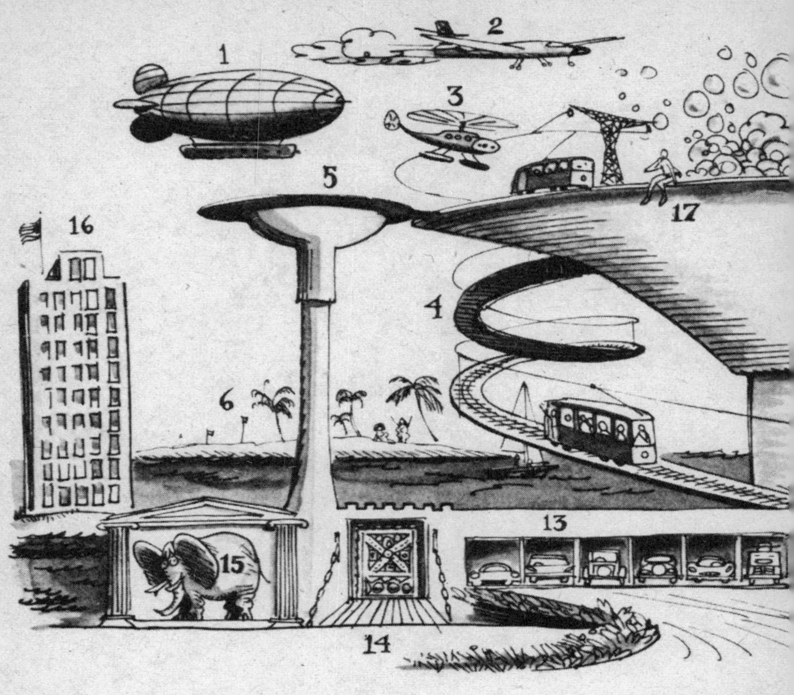

Men not only know how to make money: they know how to spend it. To free himself and his family from everyday financial worries is the ambition of every provider. Shown here is a typical cottage* fantasised by a husband hoping to come into money some day. Airship **(1)** takes visitors on a sightseeing tour. Supersonic jet **(2)** and helicopter **(3)** save cost of tickets for commercial flight. Time being of essence to the comfortably rich, tramway **(4)** provides quick transport from heliport **(5)** to main cottage. Visible in the distance is a private island **(6)** with a private eighteen-hole golf course and a private nudist colony, open all night. On top of house is swimming pool **(7)**, complete with skilled private secretaries discovered

* Wholly tax-deductible.

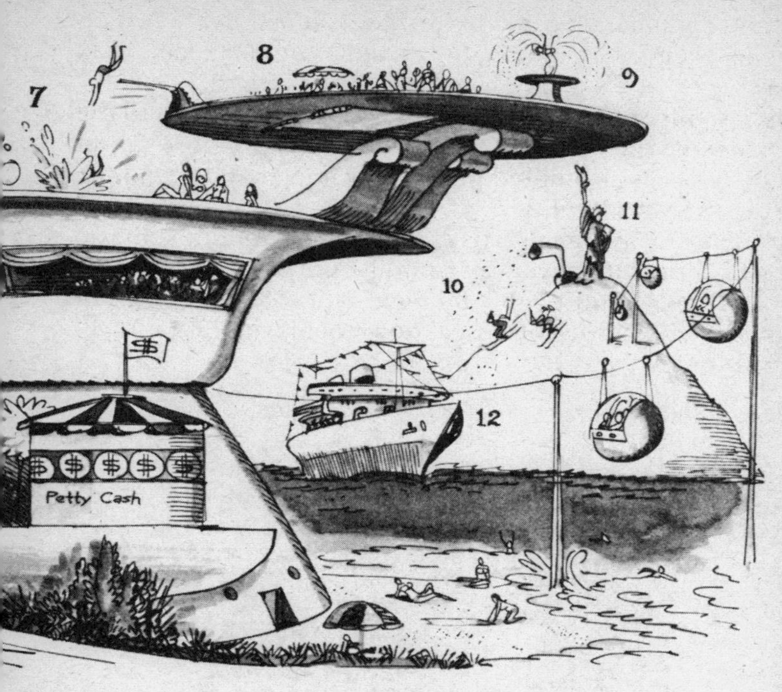

at some of the finest night clubs in the country. Terrace **(8)** is capable of supporting large group of guests but entire party can easily be dropped to the ground by means of secret hatch. Marble fountainhead **(9)** spouts alcoholic beverages. Artificial snow on artificial mountain **(10)** offers winter sports throughout year for ski enthusiasts. At the peak stands an authentic reproduction of the Statue of Liberty **(11)** to dramatize owner's gratitude to the country that was good to him. Private yacht **(12)** is for trips around the world to get away from it all. Adjacent six-door garage **(13)** is accessible through authentic drawbridge **(14).** Live elephant **(15)** is trained to perform heavy work, such as taking out the garbage. Ten-storey building **(16)** serves for servants' head-quarters. Owner **(17)** is on the terrace, stifling a yawn.

Husband's financial acumen is put to its most severe test on April 15 every year, due date for the Federal Income Tax Return.

His assignment is clear: the less money is passed on to the Government, the more he has left to spend on more useful projects. Success is limited only by his imagination, and the tax examiner's gullibility.

Rarely is the average taxpayer concerned about the moral issue of keeping money away from the Government. He is – or so he thinks – thoroughly familiar with spending habits of congressmen. His idea of a breakdown of the national budget is shown below.

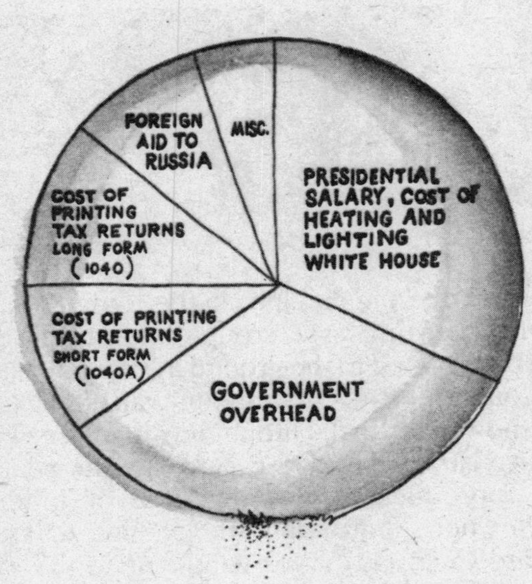

THE NATIONAL BUDGET

Be with him when he needs you most. Give him your support when he makes out his income tax return.

Form **1040** Combined with Form 1040A **US** Department of the Treasury / Internal Revenue Service

Individual Income Tax Return 1969

For the year January 1–December 31, 1969, or other taxable year beginning .... 1969, ending .... 19 ....

Please print or type

First name and initial (If joint return, use first names and middle initials of both) | Last name | Your social security number

Present home address (Number and street or rural route) | Your occupation

City, town or post office, State and ZIP code | Spouse's social security number

Enter below name and address used on your return for 1968 (if same as above write "Same"). If none filed, give reason. If changing from separate to joint or joint to separate returns, enter 1968 names and addresses. | Spouse's occupation

Name and address of employer at time of filing

Your Filing Status— (Check only one)

1 ☐ Single

2 ☐ Married filing joint return (even if only one had income)

3 ☐ Married filing separate return and spouse is also filing a return. If this item checked give spouse's social security number in space provided above and enter first name here ▶

4 ☐ Unmarried Head of Household

5 ☐ Surviving widow(er) with dependent child

6 ☐ Married filing separate return and spouse is not filing a return

Please attach Copy B of Form W-2 to back

Your Exemptions

Check boxes for exemptions which apply — Regular — 65 or over — Blind — Enter number of boxes checked ▶

7a Yourself

7b Spouse (applies only if line 2 or line 6 is checked)

8 First names of your dependent children who lived with you — Enter number ▶

9 OTHER DEPENDENTS — (a) NAME —Enter figure 1 in the last column to right for each name listed (if more space is needed, use other side) — (b) Relationship — (c) Months lived in your home. See instructions, B-2 — (d) $600 or more income? — (e) Support you furnished. If 100% write "ALL." $ — (f) Support furnished by dependent and others $ ▶

10 Total exemptions from lines 7, 8, and 9 above ▶

Your Income

11 Wages, salaries, tips, etc. (Attach Form W-2 to back. If unavailable, explain on back) — 11

12a Dividends (Total before exclusion) $ (See item 2 on 1040-1) 12b Less Exclusion $ — Balance ▶ 12c

13 Interest (Enter total here and if over $100, also list in Schedule B, Part II) — 13

14 Other income. Total from attached schedules (check schedules used—C ☐, D ☐, E ☐, F ☐) — 14

15a Total (Add lines 11, 12c, 13 & 14) $ — 15b Less Adjustments (See 1040-1) $ — Adjusted Gross Income ▶ 15c

Your Tax and Surcharge

● *If line 15c is $5,000 or more, go to Schedule T, to figure tax and surcharge. (Omit lines 16 and 17.)*

● *Go to Sch. T to figure tax and surcharge if you itemize deductions, or claim retirement income credit, foreign tax credit, or investment credit, or if you owe self employment tax or tax from recomputing prior year investment credit. (Omit lines 16 and 17.)*

● *If neither of above two items applies, go to Tax Tables instead of Sch. T. Complete lines 16, 17, & 18.*

See 1040-1 for rules under which the IRS will figure your tax and surcharge

16 Tax from Tax Table (see tables on T-2 and T-3) — 16

17 Tax surcharge on line 16 (see T-1 for tax surcharge tables) — 17

18 Enter total of lines 16 and 17 **OR** amount from Schedule T, line 18, if applicable (check if from Tax Table A ☐, B ☐, C ☐; Tax Rate Sch. ☐, Sch. D ☐, or Sch. G ☐) — 18

Please attach Check or Money Order here

Your Credits

19 Total Federal income tax withheld (attach Forms W-2 to back) — 19

20 Excess F.I.C.A. tax withheld (two or more employers—see R-2) — 20

21 ☐ Nonhighway Federal gasoline tax, Form 4136; ☐ Reg. Inv., Form 2439 — 21

22 1969 Estimated tax payments (include 1968 overpayment allowed as a credit) — 22

23 Total (add lines 19, 20, 21, and 22) — 23

Make check or money order payable to Internal Revenue Service.

Balance Due or Refund

24 If line 18 is larger than line 23, enter BALANCE DUE. Pay in full with return ——▶ 24

25 If line 23 is larger than line 18, enter OVERPAYMENT ——▶ 25

26 Line 25 to be: (a) Credited on 1970 estimated tax ▶ $; (b) Refunded ▶ $

Under penalties of perjury, I declare that I have examined this return, including accompanying schedules and statements, and to the best of my knowledge and belief it is true, correct, and complete

Sign here

▶ Your signature — Date — ▶ Signature of preparer other than taxpayer, based on all information of which he has any knowledge. — Date

▶ Spouse's signature (If filing jointly, BOTH must sign even if only one had income) — Address

Your husband – sophisticated as he is in ways of finance – probably complains about the unnecessary complexities of the current tax form. The document compels him to reveal highly confidential and non-essential information about himself, such as his income, leaving insufficient space for far more important data, such as deductible expenses.

SCHEDULE A (Form 1040)
Department of the Treasury Internal Revenue Service

US

Department of the Treasury / Internal Revenue Service

Individual Income Tax Return

Itemized Deductions

► See instructions on A–1 and A–2.
► If you use this schedule, attach it to Form 1040.

1969

Name as shown on Form 1040 | Social Security Number

Medical and dental expenses (not compensated by insurance or otherwise) for medicine and drugs, doctors, dentists, nurses, hospital care, insurance premiums for medical care, etc.

1 **One half of insurance premiums for medical care (but not more than $150)** . .
2 Medicine and drugs . . . .
3 Enter 1% of line 15c, Form 1040 . . .
4 Subtract line 3 from line 2. Enter difference (if less than zero, enter zero) . .
5 Itemize other medical and dental expenses (include balance of insurance premiums for medical care not deducted on line 1) . . . .

6 Total (add lines 4 and 5) . . . . .
7 Enter 3% of line 15c, Form 1040 . . .
8 Subtract line 7 from line 6. Enter difference (if less than zero, enter zero) . .
9 **Total deductible medical and dental expenses** (add lines 1 and 8) . . . . ►

Taxes.—Real estate . . . .
State and local gasoline . . . . . .
General sales (see sales tax tables) . .
State and local income . . . . . .
Personal property . . . .

10 **Total taxes** . . . . ►

Contributions.—Cash—including checks, money orders, etc. (Itemize)

11 Total cash contributions . . . .
12 Other than cash (see instructions on A–1 for required statement). Enter total for such items here . . . .
13 Carryover from prior years (see instructions on A–2) . . . .
14 **Total contributions** (add lines 11, 12, and 13—see instructions on A–2 for limitation) . . . . . . ►

Interest expense—Home mortgage . .
Installment purchases . . . . .
Other (Itemize) . . . .

15 **Total interest expense** . . . ►

Miscellaneous deductions for child care, alimony, union dues, casualty losses, etc. (see instructions on A–2)

16 **Total miscellaneous deductions** . ►

17 **TOTAL ITEMIZED DEDUCTIONS** (add lines 9, 10, 14, 15, and 16—enter here and on Schedule T, line 2) . ►

16—80566—1

Simplified one-page tax form with itemized deductions as a main feature gets across relevant information more effectively.

Correlation between the Dow Jones average and your husband's blood pressure.

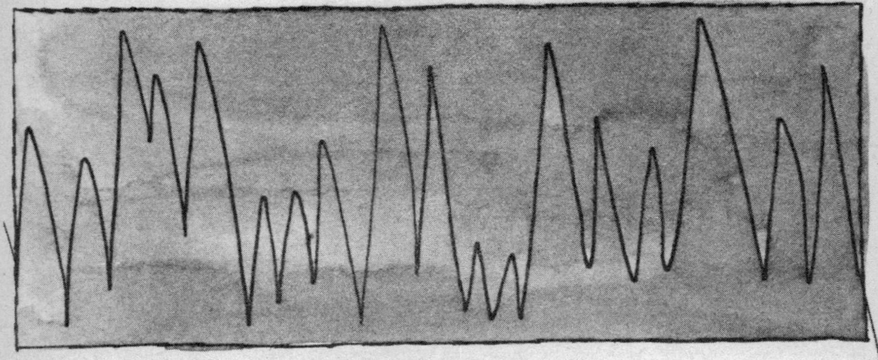

DOW JONES AVERAGE

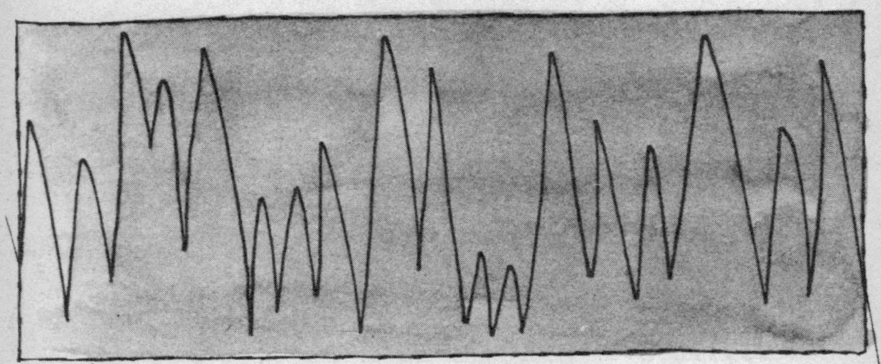

PATIENT'S BLOOD PRESSURE

Your husband's appraisal of himself as a shrewd investor is not always shared by those entrusted to keep him from losing his money. His stockbroker, for example, may have a different opinion of your husband's fiscal talents – more like the one you have come to suspect.

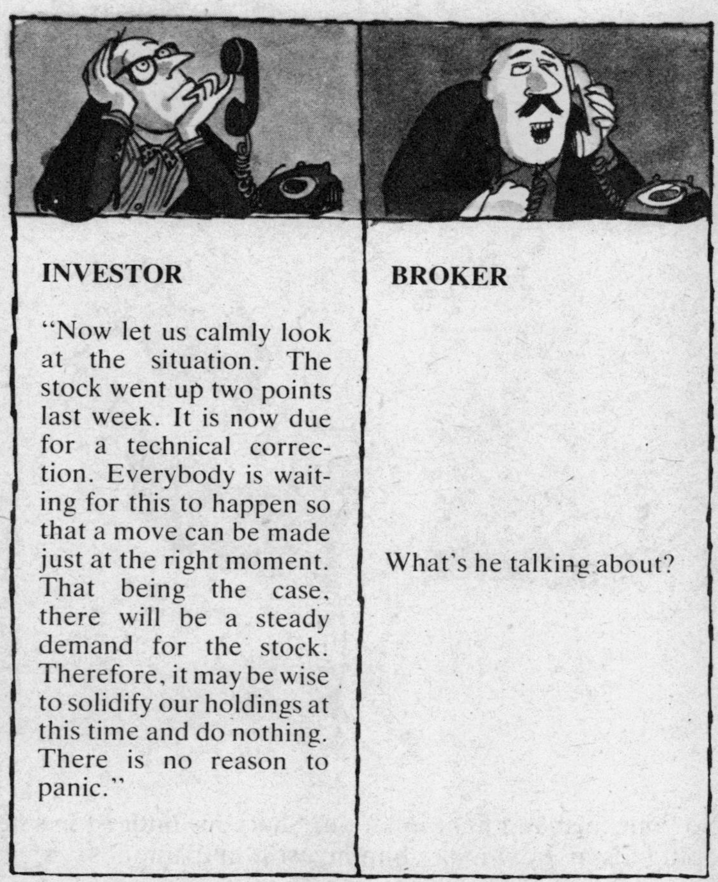

Help your husband fight inflation. Share his interest in safe-keeping his money; make him invest it in diamonds.

For small currency, go through your husband's pockets – while he is not wearing the suit, of course. For larger denominations, search lamp **(1)**, shoes **(2)**, dog's fur **(3)**, and cushion **(4)**. In the bedroom, turn over mattress **(5)**, look under painting **(6)**, knock on wall for hollow sound indicating location of hidden safe **(7)**, and while your husband is asleep, peer into his mouth.

5
THE NEUROTIC HUSBAND AND HIS SLEEPING HABITS

Interruptions may prevent your neurotic husband from sleeping through the day. Thus, he will return in the evening exhausted, collapsing on his bed. He may have a problem falling asleep, however.

Most husbands become increasingly irritated as the end of the day approaches. It occurs to them that soon they will have to share their sleeping quarters – just as a day before and a day before that – with their wives. The thought discourages them from going to sleep at all. They may choose instead to smoke cigars, read newspapers, eat, drink, walk around the block all night.

It is up to you to help your husband in getting his well-earned rest.

Facial expressions of sleeping husband reveal his subconscious thoughts – especially those concerning his marriage.

Some men talk volubly in their sleep – more than they do to their wives during the day. Listen to what your husband has to say – it may help you to understand his problems. If he is not the talkative type, watch his body movements at night; slight as they may be, they should nevertheless provide you with added insight into his unconscious. For example:

ACTION	DREAM
He jumps up and down on bed	He is dancing with his mistress
He runs around the bedroom with a wide grin on his face	He is beginning to enjoy his night out; he and his mistress are having the dance floor all to themselves
He climbs under bed	You made an appearance
He is trying to lift up the bed	He is young again
He opens the window and with a blanket thrown about his shoulder, he stands at the ledge	He is Superman
He is shadow boxing	He is asking his boss for a raise
He is kicking himself	He remembers his wedding

532
533
534
535
536

Back massage helps relieve tension, lulls him to sleep.

A quick and efficient way to put your husband to sleep.

If he snores, accept it as part of married life. Learn to appreciate the sound, listening to it as you would to a melody. Snoring is, after all, a form of music. Pursing his lips while exhaling, the snorer can imitate the warble of a bird **(1)**, bringing a touch of the outdoors into the house. From the depth of his throat come the vibrations of an accomplished opera singer **(2)**. And once he masters snoring from his diaphragm, he will be able to project the sound across the room **(3)**.

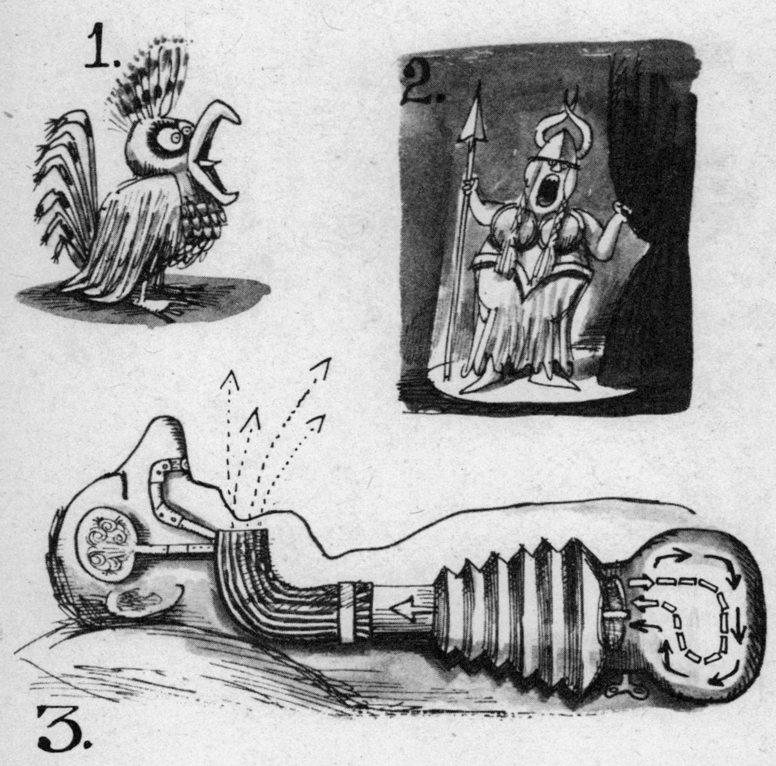

If you are musically unsophisticated, and cannot, for the life of you, derive pleasure from listening to the sound of snoring, you have no choice but to seek refuge. Putting one hand over his mouth while holding his nose with the other is one way to control his snoring. However, this may prevent him from breathing altogether. Other methods (shown below) may prove to be more practical.

Put a pillow over your head.

Put a pillow over his head.

Sleep in the living room closet.

Wake him up gently.

At certain times, you may find yourself in the same bed with your husband. This can lead to complications. Most husbands are just as neurotic in bed as they are outside of it.

Newspaper Reader turns pages rapidly – and noisily – to get to the more important news items in the sports section. Once there, he unfolds the newspaper with a sweeping gesture, covering your face with it.

Smoker disappears behind a billowing cloud before going to sleep. Only his cough tells of his whereabouts.

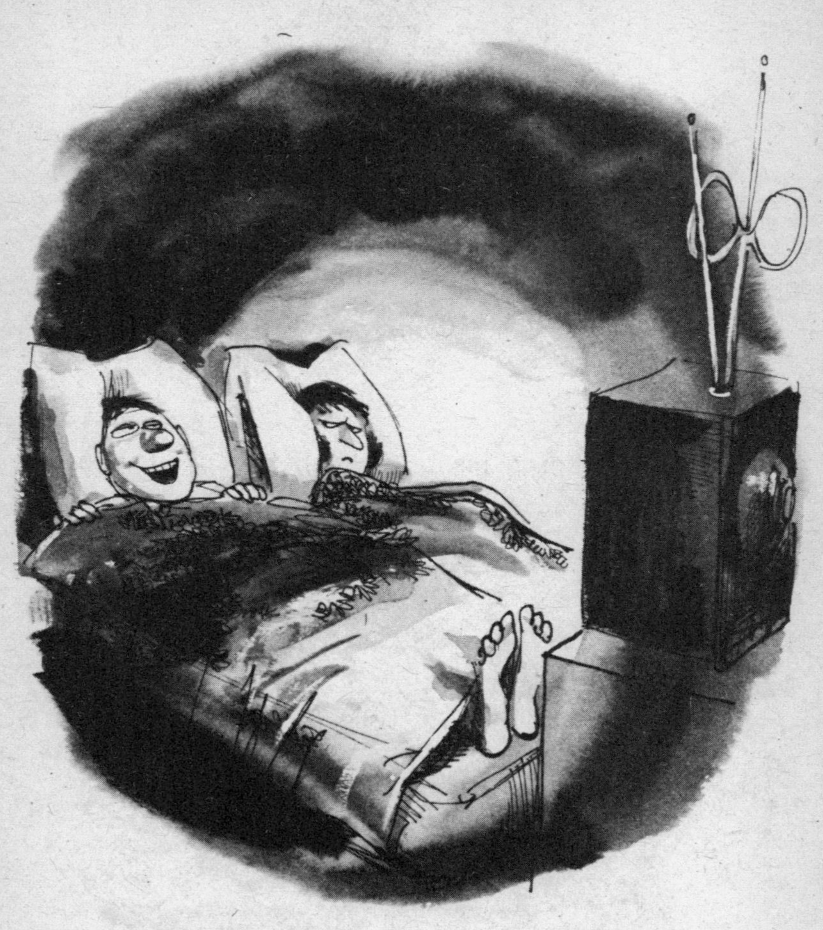

The Late-late-show Watcher gets more enjoyment out of movies when seen for the second, third, or fourth time. To make it easier for you to follow the plot, he will have a running commentary all his own.

Physical Culturist prepares for the night by limbering up.

Picknicker knows that time for breakfast is still many hours away. He is not about to go hungry in the meantime.

Ardent Lover becomes passionate several times at night. A romanticist at heart, he may try winning the affections of his companion with words prior to launching an all-out attack.

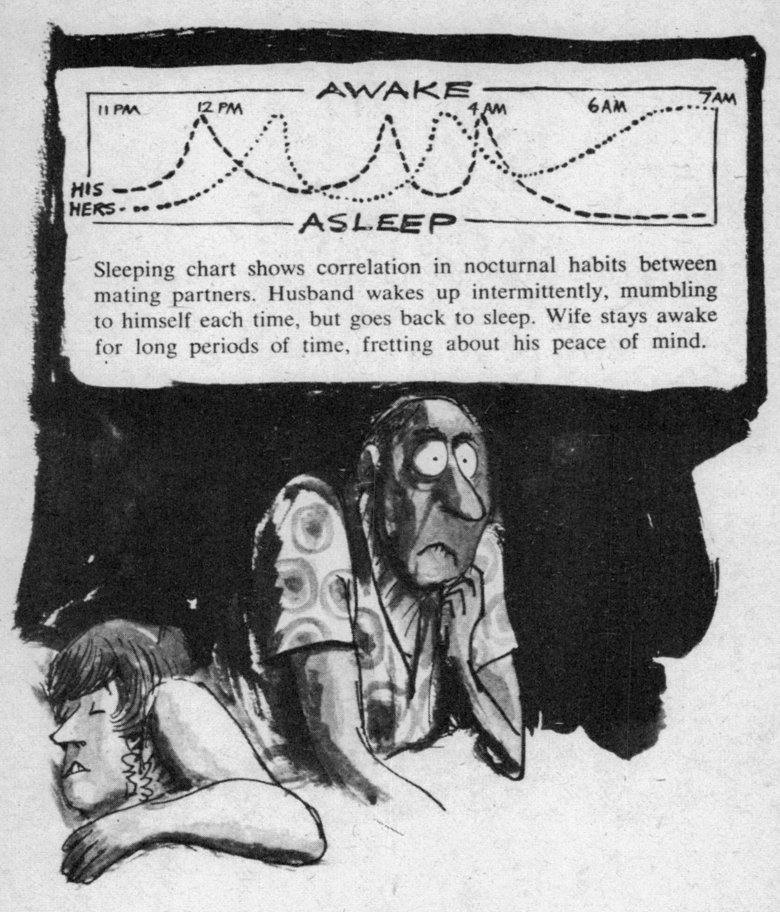

Sleeping chart shows correlation in nocturnal habits between mating partners. Husband wakes up intermittently, mumbling to himself each time, but goes back to sleep. Wife stays awake for long periods of time, fretting about his peace of mind.

The **I've-got-to-get-up-just-for-a-minute-dear Husband** alternates his night journeys between kitchen and bathroom. On his way, he may try to vault over your body — but not always successfully.

Thoughts that wake up husbands with a start:

WHAT WAS THAT?

TOMORROW WILL BE ANOTHER DAY. RIGHT?

I THINK I'LL GET MYSELF A TOMATO AND CHEESE PIZZA PIE.

IS THAT YOU, GWEN? OH, EXCUSE ME, I DIDN'T KNOW IT WAS YOU, DEAR.

IT'S DARK IN HERE.

I AM BORED.

IT'S TOO QUIET HERE.

LET'S HAVE SEPARATE VACATIONS. YOU GO AND VISIT YOUR SISTER. TAKE THE KIDS WITH YOU. I'LL STAY.

HOW LONG HAVE WE BEEN MARRIED?

TOMORROW I'LL GIVE UP SMOKING.

TOMORROW I'LL GIVE UP DRINKING.

WE'RE NOT AS YOUNG AS WE USED TO BE.

WHAT DO YOU THINK OF JIM'S WIFE?

ARE YOU ASLEEP?

Waking up a husband requires a plan of action. For best results, mix sound effects with physical stimuli. Noise level must be loud enough to bring him out of his stupor. Watch him regaining consciousness. First he will — with noticeable effort – raise his eyelids. He may even try to sit up. He will not be able to retain his posture for long of course, and fall

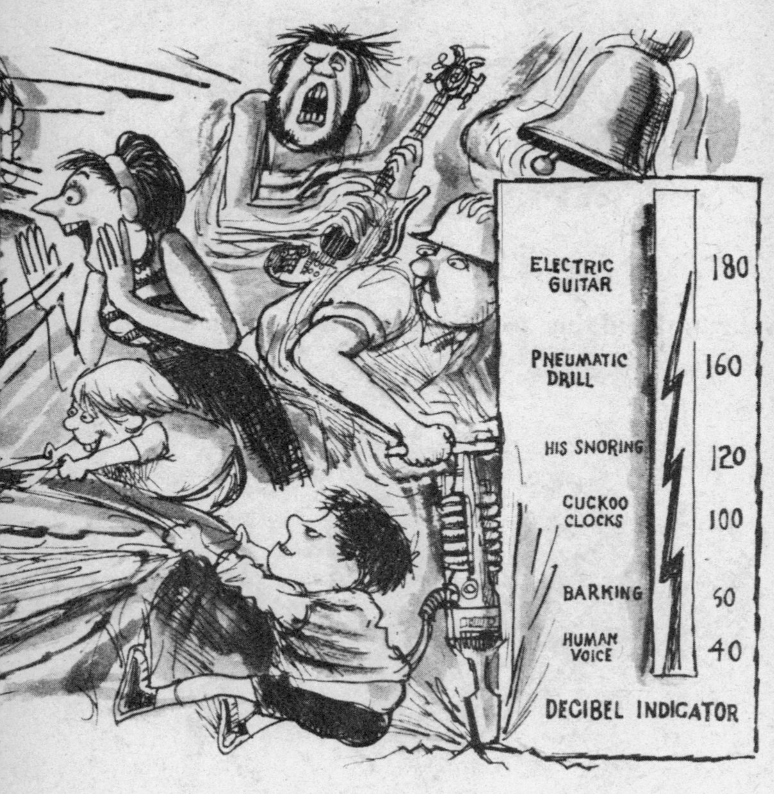

back on his pillow exhausted. Now turn your house pet loose to romp on bed. Start specially installed pneumatic drills and cuckoo clocks. Turn on cold water shower. Dispatch children. Start playing electric guitar. Sing out loud. Toll bells. Then say, "It's time to get up, dear".

Give your husband time to open *both* eyes in the morning.

Attaining vertical position (90°) calls for considerable muscular effort. Upper body is raised first. Leg is permitted to fall to the floor in search for ground. Gradually weight is shifted to the feet. Upright at last, your husband will try to walk in general direction of bathroom.

Exhausted from the ordeal of getting up in the morning, husband catches up on lost sleep in his office.

6
HOW TO TRAVEL WITH A NEUROTIC HUSBAND

Husbands like to travel. It gives them another excuse to stay away from home. Psychological studies indicate that the more the distance grows between the husband and his home, the more his disposition improves.

The only spoilsport may be the wife. For there are women who take their matrimonial vows seriously. These women believe in the concept of togetherness not only in theory but in fact. Naturally, husbands have their own opinions about the subject. It is not that they are against togetherness; on the contrary, they are all for it – provided that togetherness means they are together with a woman to whom they are not married.

Try to understand his point of view.

Husband on a business trip has an opportunity to concentrate on his work.

Husbands have reasons to want to go alone on trips, or at least without their wives. Their reasons are based on common sense. If the wife cannot understand his way of looking at things, that is her problem, not his. Here are some typical reasons:

SOMEBODY MUST STAY AT HOME WITH THE KIDS

WIFE NEEDS A REST: THE EXCITEMENT WOULD BE TOO MUCH FOR HER

IT'S A BUSINESS TRIP*

ONLY MEN ARE ALLOWED

A WOMAN'S PLACE IS AT HOME

IT'S TOO COLD TO TRAVEL THIS TIME OF THE YEAR

IT'S TOO WARM TO TRAVEL THIS TIME OF THE YEAR

ONLY SINGLE ROOMS ARE AVAILABLE AT THE HOTEL

THE TRIP IS DANGEROUS**

* "You wouldn't know what to do with yourself all day."

**"There may be health hazards such as malaria, diphtheria, sleeping sickness, typhoid fever, yaws, yellow jack, pox, septic poisoning, foot-and-mouth disease, appendicitis, locomotor ataxia, gout, dystrophy, scurvy, trichinosis, bubonic plague, the bends, athlete's foot, or any combination of these."

Camping is a favourite recreation with men who want to commune with nature. Shown here is a camping site as described by a husband trying to persuade his wife to join him on his trip.

Same camping site as seen by the wife a day after arrival.

Both husband and wife look forward to the many happy evenings they are about to spend together during holidays. However, it is not always possible to agree on just what constitutes a happy evening. The husband may be perfectly content to relax at home after a day's activity, and enjoy a meal prepared by his wife.

She would rather eat in a restaurant where someone else is doing the cooking. Having survived another day in her life, taking care of the entire family calls for celebration.

Possible compromise between husband and wife is to dress formally, have a quick dinner, and then dance to the music of crickets and bullfrogs.

Space-saving shirt-folding technique, developed by itinerant husbands.

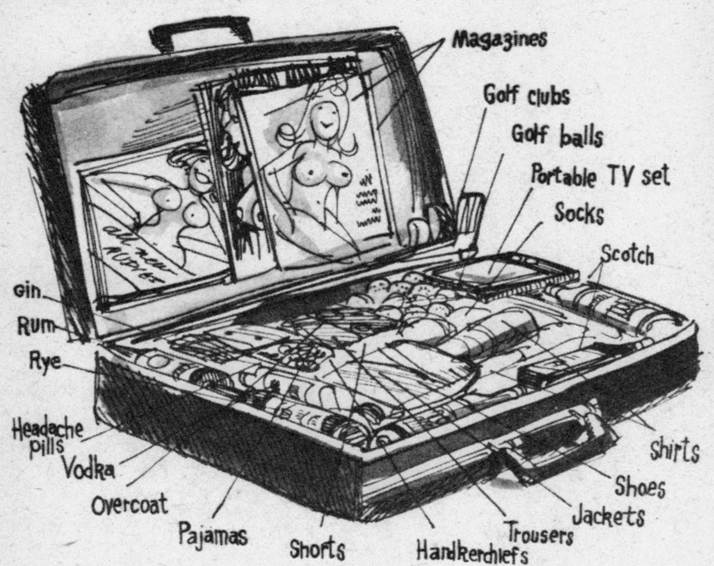

Men – more experienced in travelling than women – pack with consummate skill, efficiency, and speed. They can get more into a suitcase. They learned to economize on space by rolling everything into the shape of a ball.

Travelling by air is popular with both men and women. She enjoys the panoramic view below.

Husband enjoys the view, too.

The more the male passenger thinks about the view, the better he likes it.

It is a man's prerogative to plan ahead on a trip. Let him make all the major decisions; you make the minor ones.

Your husband may prefer to travel by car. This gives him an opportunity to prove man's mastery over machine. Shown here is the male's favourite fantasy of himself as a handler of automobiles.

Male drivers come in assorted sizes, shapes, and display wide variety of attitudes. With their hands planted firmly on the wheel, they control the destiny of fellow passengers in the car.

Nocturnal Driver uses automobile to conquer the unknown. Pretending he is awake, he guides the vehicle down the darkest of roads with consummate skill.

Perfectionist insists that an automobile should be inspected several times a day, preferably at each filling station. Occasionally, he may even ask for a few gallons of gas.

Commander-in-Chief plans his moves carefully. At the end of each day, gains are totalled up; family gets briefed on forthcoming manoeuvres.

Packing Authority takes pride in his skill in making a van out of an ordinary passenger automobile. The heavier the load, the greater the challenge.

Mother's Helper is able to give advice to his wife even while asleep.

As a main source of travel information, the Shortcut Expert uses airline maps in driving his automobile. If nothing else, they prove his theory: The shortest distance between two points is a straight line.

Shortcut Expert knows how to save distance – if not time. Have your compass ready.

7
HOW TO MAKE A NEUROTIC HUSBAND FEEL MORE RELAXED

Husbands often go through periods of acute depression in the later part of their marriage; say, a day or two after the marriage ceremony. Your responsibility is to bring joy back into his life.

The easiest way for you to fight your husband's depression would be, of course, to pack your belongings and leave. Instantly, there will be an improvement in his outlook on life. However, this solution offers only a temporary relief; your husband will soon discover that during your absence there is no one to cook for him.

Actually, your physical presence is not the only problem he has. His difficulties are more deep-seated than that. He is beginning to realize that he is not what he used to be; he is getting – by some quirk of nature – exactly a year older every year.

As the years pass, you – and your husband – will become increasingly aware of certain physical changes that go with age. These changes are particularly noticeable at the top of his head **(A),** in the area of his abdomen **(B),** and his girlfriends **(C).**

To make him feel young, look young.

Dancing helps in boosting his morale. A little fun will make your husband forget about his advancing years. Encourage

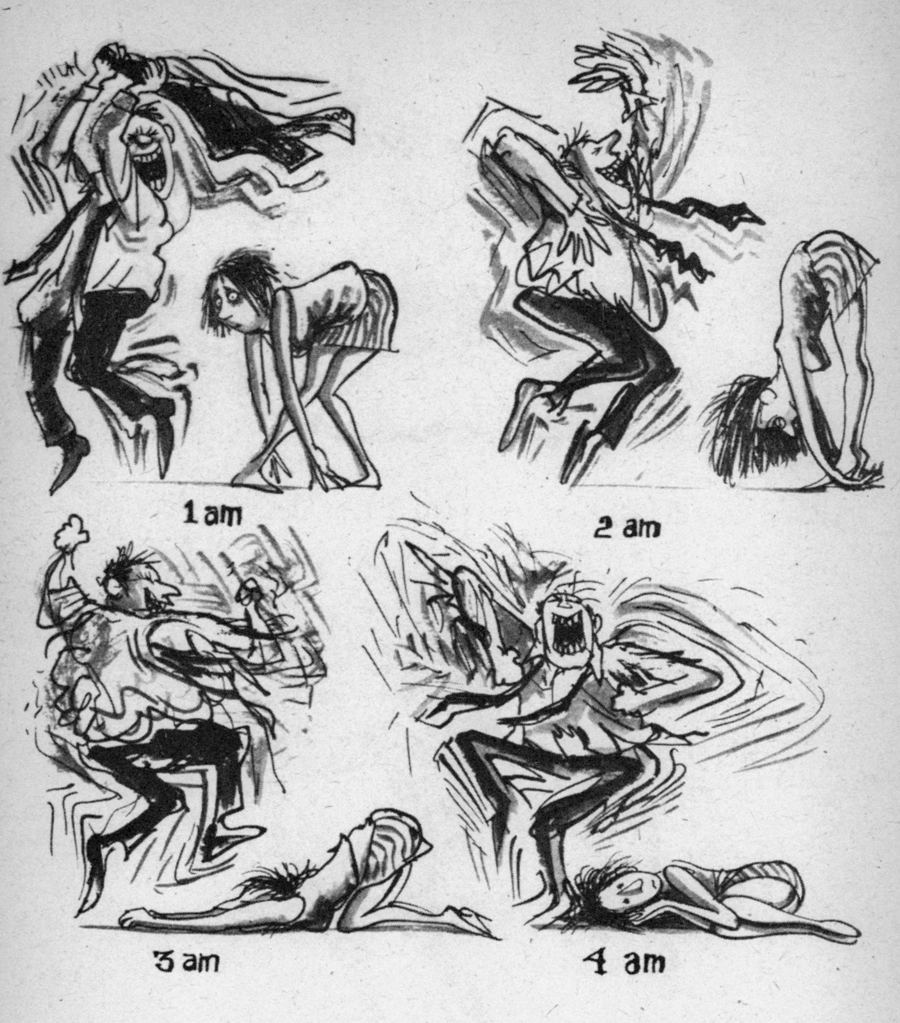

him to follow you to the dance floor. Then stay with him as long as you can hold out.

Exercise will make him feel better. Join him.

To develop arm and shoulder muscles, lift weights.

Have him take you along on his new motorcycle.

Share with him the adventure of deep-sea diving.

As your husband gets older, there may be a decline not only in his athletic prowess but his interest in love-making as well.

This is particularly true if the marriage is a lasting one, going on for as long as a year or more.

You must not blame yourself for this development. Outside interests may demand much of his energy, making him understandably tired and irritable at evenings. Such outside interests may include drinking, playing poker with friends, or dinners with his favourite girlfriend.

Fortunately, there is much you can do to help him. You can build up his self-confidence by making him feel wanted.

1. Give him a kiss.

2. Give him a hug.

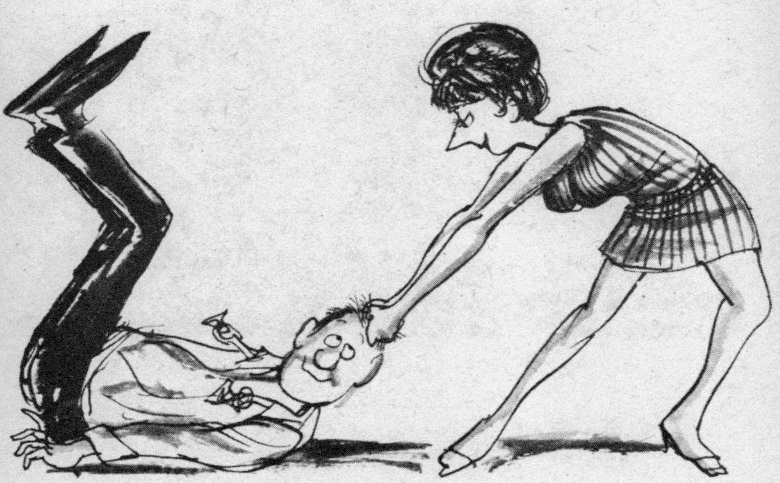

3. Gentle persuasion will make him follow you into the bedroom.

19

If your husband is a golf enthusiast, be glad that he found an outside interest. It will give you an opportunity to indulge in your own hobbies for weeks at a time.

A nap now and then relaxes a man. He will regain consciousness after the meal – when it's time to go home.

To make him feel better, burp your husband after meals.

Many wives worry when they discover that their husband has a mistress or two on the side. They think that because the other women are younger, more beautiful, and more desirable in every way, his masculine ego will make him prefer them to her. This, of course, does not have to be the case at all, provided you handle the situation calmly.

While you may not be as young, beautiful, and desirable as his mistresses, you can make an impression on your husband in other ways. You have other virtues; like, for example, your attorney.

Lawyers are very responsive to the plight of their female clients complaining about errant husbands, for their legal training allows them to size up the situation objectively. A lawyer knows that it costs money to obtain a divorce and most of this – if the case is handled properly – is going to end up with him. For this reason, he will make every effort to listen to you, particularly when the conversation turns to your husband's earning capacity.

Meeting with your attorney will give you a better understanding of your marriage. The same goes for your husband.

There may even be flowers in your room for the first time in years after your visit to a lawyer . . .

and kisses . . .

and gifts . . .

And so you will live happily ever after. At least for a while.